FIFTY
BAGS
THAT
CHANGED
THE
WORLD

DESIGN MUSEUM
FIFTY
BAGS
THAT
CHANGED
THE
WORLD

 conran
OCTOPUS

FIFTY
BAGS

FIFTY
BAGS

The bag is at once the simplest, the most complicated and the most emotion-laden of accessories. It is *simple* because since time immemorial it has served as a vital tool for living, even survival – there is evidence that one of the bag genres featured in this book, the backpack, was used by our nomadic forebears. It is *complicated* because the bag has developed and fulfilled so many different functions that its diversity is almost bewildering – we would scarcely recognize the generic relationship at all between, say, a nylon bicycle pannier and a calf-leather Gucci or Moschino.

Finally, it is *emotion-laden* because in one of its key manifestations, the handbag, it can be deeply expressive of a woman's life – serving as a companion, a receptacle of secrets, a status object and a means of self-display. This investment of emotion explains, and to some degree justifies, the handbag's key place in contemporary fashion culture, as well as the extraordinary 'It bag' explosion of the 1990s and 2000s. The handbag, it seems, has become an icon of our postmodern globalized culture – and, like all icons, is alternately venerated and contested, desired and dismissed.

The handbag, however, is by no means the only kind of bag that the Design Museum wishes to celebrate in this book. At least as much design 'capital' goes into the development of, say, an effective army rucksack as goes into a beautiful Fendi baguette. It is, above all, the endless diversity and ingenuity of bag design that are on display here.

A woman's companion: whether an Orla Kiely tote (see page 2) or a classic Chanel 2.55 (right), the handbag is much, much more than a mere receptacle.

GLADSTONE'S BUDGET BOX   c.1860

Every year on Budget day the Chancellor of the Exchequer – the UK's finance minister – stands on the doorstep of his official London home, 11 Downing Street, and raises a battered red briefcase towards the waiting press. The case's worn, dog-eared appearance is meant to reassure – the age-old traditions live on – but in reality most people look upon its annual appearance with gloom. For the Chancellor is about to give his Budget speech to Parliament and that always means bad news for someone.

This famous briefcase, first used by William Gladstone when he served as Chancellor in 1859–66, is, technically speaking, a box, one of a whole family of red or black despatch boxes used by the British government to transport classified documents. The Budget box's body is made of pine and covered with scarlet ram's leather, while the inside is lined with lead – originally intended to make the box sink in case of disaster at sea – and sombre black satin. The case has an oddity shared by all despatch boxes in that it opens at the opposite side to the handle, making it impossible to carry without its first being locked.

The original Budget box had been used by all but two Chancellors since Gladstone. Sadly, owing to its fragility, its last appearance was for the Budget of June 2010, after which it was 'retired' to the Cabinet War Rooms.

The battered budget box has been used by dozens of British Chancellors of the Exchequer since 1860 and is one of the most potent symbols of the British government.

8

CARPETBAG

1860s

During the upheavals of the American Civil War (1861–5) and the Reconstruction period (1865–77) that followed, the carpetbag became the symbol of a nation on the move. This cheap, hardwearing and capacious bag could be easily packed and carried, and was a ubiquitous sight at stagecoach halts, railway stations and steamboat jetties as people fled the ravages of war or wandered in search of new opportunities. Its appearance was a sure sign of a stranger in town, and during the Reconstruction the derogatory term 'carpetbagger' was used to describe a profiteer from the North who came to exploit the prostrate, post-bellum South.

The carpetbag was the great American bag of the nineteenth century.

As the name implies, carpetbags were constructed from odd bits of used carpet stretched across a metal frame. Often made by saddlers, they could be sold for around a dollar (roughly $20–$25 in today's money). A commentator in the 1880s described the bag thus: 'The old-fashioned carpetbag is still unsurpassed by any, where rough wear is the principal thing to be studied. Such a bag, if constructed of good Brussels carpeting and unquestionable workmanship, will last a lifetime, provided always that a substantial frame is used.' Some of the more rough-and-ready carpetbags served a double purpose: unlatched and unfolded, they became a travel blanket, perfect for a long, cold night in a draughty railway carriage.

The bag of the opportunist though it may historically be, the carpetbag endures to this day. No longer made from carpet, it still retains the rich Oriental patterning of its forebear and is valued as a strong and stylish travel bag.

SELF-OPENING SACK

1883
Charles Stilwell

In 2008 New York's Museum of Modern Art invited the Brazilian contemporary artist Vik Muniz to curate a show of his personal favourites from the collection. One of his more unusual choices – which was startlingly juxtaposed with a Giacometti sculpture – was a pleated brown paper bag of the kind that millions of Americans use for carrying home their groceries. Another typical piece of conceptual art then, a neo-Duchampian ready-made? Not a bit of it, for this unassuming object was the 'Self-Opening Sack', or SOS, patented by Charles Stilwell in 1883 and a landmark in US design history.

It is perhaps an exaggeration to claim that the nineteenth century invented shopping, but certainly during this time the habit really took off. No wonder, then, that the century also saw a series of innovations in the development of the shopping bag. While Francis Wolle invented the first paper-bag machine in 1852, the honour of being the 'father' of the modern grocery bag is usually bestowed on the Philadelphia printer Charles Stilwell (1845–1919).

Stilwell's principal concern was that his bag should stand up on its own, so he introduced side pleats that added enormously to its structural strength. A simple-enough device, no doubt, but it was this unfussy design solution that made the bag an enduring classic. You will never look at a grocery bag in the same way again.

The paper shopping bag remained a stalwart of the grocery trade well into the 1970s, until the 'triumph' of the plastic carrier bag (see page 46).

12

SADDLEBAG

1880s

Whether you were a cowboy or an Indian, the saddlebag was an indispensable item out on the plains, something in which to carry food, medicines and tools. A Native American rawhide saddlebag was flat, like an envelope, and was decorated with vivid patterns and long fringes; a cowboy's was typically plainer and more utilitarian, with a straightforward buckle flap. Most saddlebags came in pairs, hanging at the back of the saddle, although smaller, single bags were sometimes carried at the pommel (front) and cantle (back) as well.

The classic pouch-like saddlebag is a good example of form meeting function. Its narrow, almost semicircular body fits neatly against the horse's flanks – any longer and it would risk impeding the horse's movement – and the leather has to be thick and sturdy enough to withstand the constant scuffing and chafing. Surprisingly perhaps, despite its strong silhouette and iconic status in the history of the American West, the saddlebag has had only minimal influence on the fashion bag. One exception was John Galliano's witty reinterpretation of the bag for Christian Dior in 2001, which turned the fashion house's classic 'D' logo into stirrups.

Right: The ultimate cowboy, John Wayne, on horseback on set for a film from the 1960s. Below: The saddlebag is the product of the age-old relationship between man and horse, perfectly designed and adapted for long rides out in the open country.

DOCTOR'S BAG

early 1900s

In the days when physicians used to make house calls, the doctor's bag was an indispensable piece of equipment, as precious as a stethoscope or thermometer, and just as emblematic of a physician's trade. A doctor had to take everything with him and so his 'emergency bag', as it was also called, needed to be large and well structured, with plenty of internal compartments. It had to be hardwearing, too – ready for that night-time dash in a horse-drawn buggy – and strong enough to withstand a jolt or two without breaking the bottles and vials inside.

In shape the doctor's bag resembled the Gladstone – the ubiquitous portmanteau, or travel bag, of the late Victorian era. Constructed from a sturdy frame, stiff leather and handsome brass fittings, the doctor's bag unlocked at the top to reveal two deep compartments on either side of the central, leather-lined mouth. In this large central compartment were all manner of pockets and straps for holding syringes and medicines, as well as enough space for notebooks and papers, and items of more cumbersome equipment.

As the proud badge of the profession, the doctor's bag was typically expensive. At the turn of the twentieth century, one large American version was marketed at $25, which is roughly $650 in today's money. No wonder, then, that such bags were often given as a gift from father to son setting out on his chosen career.

The classic doctor's bag (below) is not just for doctors: a district nurse (right) checks on her equipment while out on her rounds.

STEAMER BAG

c.1901
Louis Vuitton

The Louis Vuitton brand – today synonymous with high-end, conspicuous luxury – was already famous back in the late nineteenth century. Founded in 1854 by a former *malletier* (trunk maker) to the French Empress Eugénie, the company responded to a burgeoning demand for practical yet luxurious luggage during the first great golden age of international travel. This was the era of long-distance trains such as the Orient Express and the palatial steamships that crisscrossed the Atlantic. Among Louis Vuitton's earliest innovations was the grey Trianon trunk with its flat top, which allowed for easier stacking than the traditional curved top of other trunks of the time.

In 1901 the company introduced the simple canvas and leather steamer bag, whose squat, squarish proportions were based on the mailbags then used in the Americas. Here was a bag that could be hung on the back of a cabin door, carried around on deck – the first-class one, of course – or stored away in the hold inside one of Louis Vuitton's famous packing cases. Vuitton's signature Monogram canvas, first introduced in 1896, was here eschewed for bolder branding in the form of a black 'V' against the colours of the French flag – more easily identifiable, no doubt, in the hurly-burly of embarkation.

By the early 1900s, even before the age of commercial aviation, travel had gone global, and so had Louis Vuitton luggage. Its stores could be found in almost every major port of call – from New York to Alexandria and from Buenos Aires to Bombay.

The art of travel. During the late nineteenth century Louis Vuitton led the way in producing luxury baggage for the European and American elite. Versions of this steamer bag, dating from about 1901, are still made today.

US ARMY M-1910 HAVERSACK

Some bags are all about luxury, others about practicality. And both kinds – despite the now very tired Modernist mantra 'Form follows function' – can be excellent examples of design.

When it comes to practicality, little can beat the US Army's M-1910 haversack. Introduced in 1910 and used in World War I, it was to remain standard equipment for American infantrymen (with only slight amendments after 1928) until the very end of World War II. In essence, the M-1910 was a simple sheet of khaki-coloured canvas that folded around the contents, with a buttoned flap to close it and two broad shoulder straps, which for stability also attached to a web belt worn around the waist. The bag carried everything the soldier needed for life out in the field. Inside were his bedding, clothing and personal effects, while outside, attached by a system of loops and rings, were the tools of his trade – a bayonet sheath and a short, squat shovel for digging trenches. At the back of the pack was a buttoned-down 'meat-can pouch' to hold the soldier's rations.

The origins of the haversack itself are even less glamorous, but just as down to earth. The German dialect word *Habersack* referred to the feeding bags cavalrymen carried for their horses, although by the late eighteenth century the word had come to be used for soldiers' kitbags as well.

Two American soldiers wearing the M-1910 haversack during World War I.

METAL MESH BAG   c.1925

Bags and purses made from metal mesh were first made in the early nineteenth century, but were objects of absolute luxury. The intricate mesh was made by gold- and silversmiths, and suspended from a frame studded with precious stones. The metal mesh bag came back into fashion in the late nineteenth century, when exquisite tiny purses were worn hanging from the waist in a faux-medieval style.

The invention of a mechanized process for making metal mesh in 1908 meant that such 'trinkets' became much more affordable, and by the mid-1920s metal mesh bags and purses were a staple part of the flapper's evening wardrobe. Elongated bell-shaped silhouettes, lacy or zigzag fringes, and Art Deco or 'Egyptian'-style clasps were all common features, adding just the right note of jazzy sparkle to a long-fringed Charleston dress. The leading maker was the US company Whiting and Davis, whose designs were commissioned from some of the leading couturiers of the day, Paul Poiret and Elsa Schiaparelli among them.

Shimmering and fluid, light as a feather and tough as nails, the 1920s metal mesh bag had all the ingredients for the perfect evening accessory. Here was a bag to match the moonlight on a late-night promenade in St-Tropez.

Right: This French metal mesh bag features a silver frame and a black-and-white enamelled clasp in an 'Egyptian' style. Below: This bell-shaped German example, with its 'Greek key' pattern, was typical of many metal mesh bags of the early twentieth century.

BEADWORK EVENING BAG

Maria Likarz-Strauss

Founded in 1903 and closed in 1932, the Austrian Wiener Werkstätte (Vienna Workshops) was one of the great birthplaces of modern design. Under the auspices of Josef Hoffmann (1870–1956), the workshops pioneered functionalist designs that bridged the divide between manufactured products and craft-based traditions. While the Wiener Werkstätte are famous for their ground-breaking architecture, interiors and furniture, their influence on the development of textile design is less well known. It was largely owing to the work of Hoffmann's pupil Maria Likarz-Strauss (1893–1956).

A bag for the Jazz Age. The Austrian Maria Likarz-Strauss here transposes her striking, vibrant textile designs to an elegant beadwork evening bag.

This exquisite beaded evening bag is a beautiful example of Likarz-Strauss's work. The result of hours of patient threading and sewing, beadwork had been a staple of the home-made bags of the nineteenth century. Here the designer updated the genre for the industrial age, but without sacrificing its intimate charm. Minuscule beads are used to create a vibrant abstract design that both looks back to the decorative work of the Viennese painter Gustav Klimt (1862–1918) and reflects the high tide of Art Deco.

Nothing could be simpler than this bag. Domestic, demure yet modern, this is remote indeed from the more showy evening bags that were popular at this time. Every design decade has its contrasts.

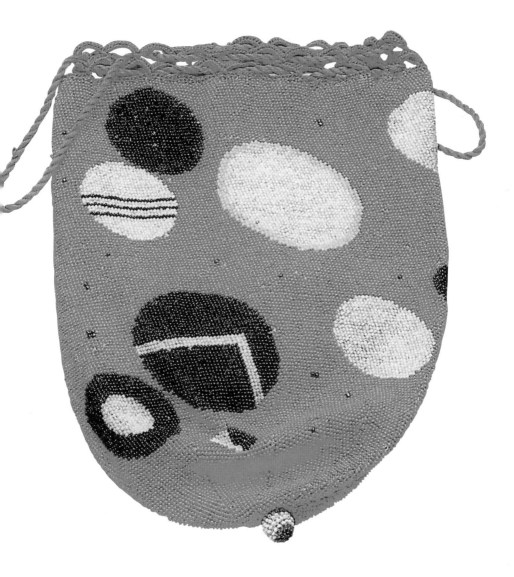

NEWSBOY BAG

c.1935

The barely adolescent newsboy – with his peaked and pillowed 'newsboy cap' and heavy, oversized 'newsboy bag' – was one of the iconic figures of the American street scene in the late nineteenth and early twentieth centuries, when the shrill cry of 'Extra! Extra!' was the insistent litany associated with every homeward-bound commute. In New York, at the time of the famous Newsboys Strike of 1899, at least five thousand newsboys plied the city streets and avenues. Although they provided a vital service – circulating news in what was then the world's largest democracy – the boys were often considered to be little better than vagrants.

The newsboy's scruffy canvas bag was a vital tool of his trade, as vital, indeed, as his unpolished hobnailed boots. Little more than a capacious canvas envelope, with a long, strong strap and a flap to keep out rain, it was issued by the newspapers and bore the newspaper name printed prominently on the side.

By the post-war years, child labour laws and rising prosperity had brought about the demise of the downtown newsboy, but the newsboy bag lived on – in the waterproof variant used by enterprising teenagers on suburban paper routes and in the scruffy, ink-stained bags favoured by university students. The messenger bag (see page 64), of course, is another of the newsboy bag's contemporary cousins.

A British newspaper boy delivering the *Daily Herald* in 1935. The 'newsboy bags' could be almost as big as the young boys who carried them.

HALLIBURTON CASE

1938
Halliburton

Think Tarantino-era John Travolta in shades and you have something of the hard-edged sex appeal of this most famous of attaché cases. That said, the Halliburton really does not need such comparisons – it is, after all, a Hollywood star in its own right. In crime capers such as *Ocean's Eleven* and hit TV series such as *Lost* and *24*, its mere appearance onscreen suggests that high-grade shenanigans are afoot and cranks up the tension no end. What on earth, we wonder, is inside? A sniper rifle, bundles of $100 bills… or just a businessman's lunchtime sandwiches?

The Halliburton's prototype was designed for the American oilman Erle P. Halliburton (1892–1957), who needed a case that would withstand the wear and tear of long truck journeys through the Texan outback. Halliburton was impressed enough to put the case into manufacture, but a few years after World War II he sold the company to the metal-fabrication company Zero, which has continued to make the Zero Halliburton ever since.

The modern Zero Halliburton is a portable fortress and well-nigh impervious to even the heaviest blows or blasts. No less than two tons of aircraft-grade aluminium goes into the manufacture of every case, and its arduous production process includes a heat treatment that rises to 538°C (1,000°F). Perfect, in short, for throwing out of that exploding helicopter.

Right and below: Cool, chic, impregnable… If one of the primary purposes of the bag is to provide protection for its contents, then the Halliburton case is probably the ultimate bag.

BICYCLE PANNIERS

From the golden age of cycling in the 1890s onwards, cyclists have sought ways to adapt their bicycles in order to carry cycling paraphernalia and personal possessions. The basket over the handlebars was one solution, but this, though handy for shopping, was hardly practical for routine commutes or long-distance touring, where capacity and protection from the elements were crucial. Here the pairs of saddlebags used on horses (see page 14) were the natural inspiration – in its early days, after all, the bicycle was widely known as the 'mechanical horse' – and so the bicycle pannier was born.

Modern panniers are usually attached to the rear of the bicycle, hooked onto the luggage rack by an elastic mechanism or a latch; occasionally another pair of panniers is carried at the front as well. Panniers are usually made from waterproof canvas or nylon, thus protecting the contents from the rain. Contemporary versions for commuters are made for carrying laptops and office clothes.

The messenger bag (see page 64) used by couriers is yet another solution to the problem of the bicycle-adapted bag.

A woman on her bicycle in the place de l'Opéra, Paris, in 1945 has a pair of simple canvas panniers. Now that the bicycle is the 'green' city transport, perhaps the pannier will make a comeback.

GAS-MASK BAG

c.1940

Imagine scrabbling in your handbag not for a lipstick or tissue, but for a gas mask! At the beginning of World War II there was a very real fear in Britain and on the Continent that poison gas would be used against civilians. During the 1930s Nazi Germany had developed the deadly nerve gases tabun and sarin, and there were disturbing memories of the mustard gas used against soldiers in World War I. Accordingly, at the outbreak of war, the British government issued every civilian with a gas mask, distributing some 38 million in all.

Propaganda posters ordered civilians to carry the gas mask everywhere. The masks came in a plain square cardboard box, with instructions on the inside lid, and sporting a long adjustable strap. Initially at least, women were much more assiduous than men in carrying these unprepossessing little boxes around with them, but very quickly they tried to make them a more agreeable part of their wardrobe. One solution – the cheapest – was to decorate them, covering them with fabric or painting them a colour.

Some women went further, discarding the boxes altogether and buying the specially adapted handbags that almost at once began to appear in department stores. In some instances, such handbags featured a hidden compartment at the bottom of the bag in which to store the mask. Fortunately such a finicky arrangement was never put to the test. The bags and the little cardboard boxes were soon stored away and forgotten for the rest of the war.

At the beginning of World War II the cardboard gas-mask box made a curious addition to a woman's ensemble. No wonder, then, that those who could afford to bought specially adapted leather handbags.

HOPALONG CASSIDY LUNCHBOX

1950
Aladdin Industries

During the early 1950s Hopalong Cassidy was the hero of a hugely popular American TV series – a clean-cut cowboy who never swore and who spread wholesome American values throughout the West. Its star, William Boyd (1895–1972), who owned the rights to the name, was quick to capitalize on the success of the series, licensing a welter of 'Hoppy'-themed merchandise, from roller skates and wristwatches to a humble children's lunchbox.

The lunchbox had been a staple of American life since the mid-nineteenth century – a phenomenon of the industrial age in which workers had to eat their lunch in the workplace. Early versions were essentially small woven baskets, but more durable tin (and later aluminium) versions quickly became the norm. During the 1920s and 1930s manufacturers increasingly marketed products directly at children, and in 1935 it was Disney's Mickey Mouse who inevitably became the first licensed character to appear on the side of a children's lunchbox.

The red-and-blue Hoppy lunchbox was a runaway success. Priced at $2.39, some 600,000 units were sold in the first year alone. The eventual fate of the children's metal lunchbox was less happy. In 1972 the Florida legislature – and subsequently those of other states – banned the metal boxes because children had been using them in playground fights. Hopalong Cassidy would never have approved of such behaviour.

Right: 'Down the trail the cowboy way,' went the theme-tune lyrics of *The Hopalong Cassidy Show* (1949–54). The Hopalong lunchbox (here shown with its accompanying vaccum flask) became a must-have for American schoolchildren of the early 1950s. Below: An advertisement showing other lunchboxes produced by Aladdin Industries.

HATS OFF TO MOM FOR

HER WHOLESOME LUNCHES

AND THE WONDERFUL KITS

(AND KIDS) SHE PUTS 'EM IN!

SCHOOL LUNCH KITS AND MATCHING ½-PINT VACUUM BOTTLES

SCHOOLBOY SATCHEL

The satchel is perhaps the bag we most strongly associate with childhood. Already in Shakespeare we find its classic image, so evocative of that blend of innocence and delinquency of our schooldays: 'Then the whining school-boy, with his satchel / And shining morning face, creeping like a snail / Unwillingly to school.'

As this quote from *As You Like It* (first performed in 1600) suggests, the satchel is a very old type of bag. Its name means nothing more than 'small bag', and its origins probably lie in the huntsman's game bag of medieval times. In Britain the school satchel was last widely used in the 1950s, when it was part of the traditional school uniform, along with the school tie, peaked cap, shorts and blazer. A repository for dog-eared books, inky pens, half-sucked gobstoppers (jawbreakers) and last year's conkers (horse chestnuts), the satchel was becoming antiquated by the 1960s. Eventually it would give way to a contemporary variation (see page 68) and the trendier 'street' alternative, the messenger bag (see page 64).

The form itself, however – butter-soft leather, buckled flap, and long strap worn diagonally across the shoulder – has influenced many a contemporary bag, from the manbag of the late 1990s to the woman's daysack of 2010 (see pages 80 and 104).

A British schoolboy in the 1950s with his smart new satchel looks none too happy about the prospect of a return to school.

TWA AIRLINE BAG   c.1950

The decade of the 1950s was the golden age of air travel. More and more people were taking to the skies, but not so many that it had lost its aura of glamour and sophistication. By 1955 more American citizens were travelling by plane than by train, and by the end of the decade the transatlantic flight had largely replaced the ocean-liner crossing. This was the age of impeccably groomed stewardesses – those starlets of the sky – and passengers dressed up for the occasion, too.

What more appropriate way to complete an ensemble than to carry an airline bag on board? Mass-produced though they might be, these simple, practical bags instantly conveyed cool cosmopolitanism. They usually came in a standard form and size (rectangular body, adjustable strap and zipped side pocket) – what differed was the company livery, turning them into mobile advertisements. Many a Hollywood actress was photographed at an airport arrivals lounge clutching a PanAm or TWA airline bag with the company logo prominently on display.

Air travel has long since lost its novelty, and onboard bags are now just another thing to worry about in the fraught business of flying. Back on the ground, however, adding a vintage 1950s airline bag to a contemporary outfit can lend a witty note of kitsch retro glamour.

American figure skater Carol Heiss waves from the boarding stairs of a TWA (Trans World Airlines) plane at Idlewild Airport (later John F. Kennedy Airport), New York, in 1958. In the 1950s the airline bag was synonymous with cosmopolitan glamour.

WILARDY ROCKET

1953
Will Hardy

A hard plastic handbag may seem something of a kitsch curiosity today, but back in the United States of the 1950s Will Hardy's extravagant yet durable designs were all the rage. Plastic was still the glamorous material of the future, and Lucite – or polymethyl methacrylate, to give it its non-trademarked name – was the *crème de la crème* of the plastics world.

Through the 1950s Hardy produced a series of sleek, tough Lucite bags under the company name of Wilardy, of which the brightest star was undoubtedly the capsule-shaped Rocket. Their sensual curves, rich, glossy colours and lavish decoration (rhinestones and mother-of-pearl were frequent embellishments) made them must-have accessories for starlets and society dames. The bags were practical, too: not only were they capacious enough to carry hair rollers as well as makeup, but also the slick 'click release' on the hinged lids was legendary.

Wilardy's bags were expensive – they could cost as much as a month's rent – because they were handcrafted. But by the end of the decade the development of injection moulding had led to a flood of copies, and the Lucite handbag quickly lost its chic. Today, though, a bona fide Wilardy is eminently collectable, and a few fashion houses such as Chanel have even issued contemporary interpretations. Who says that fashion does not endure?

Plastic chic. With its sleek elliptical shape, the Wilardy Rocket was the undoubted star of the Wilardy range and came in a variety of colours and forms. These stardust and pearl, gold dust and black, and gold dust intricately decorated Rockets achieve a kind of lyrical transparency that belies the material from which they are made.

2.55 BAG

1955
Coco Chanel

Rarely has a bag come with so much … well, baggage. This luxurious quilted shoulder bag has become as synonymous with the Chanel brand as those two other great fashion icons, the little black dress and the tweed suit. Unlike those two garments – products of Chanel's salad days in the 1920s and 1930s – the 2.55 was a star product of the designer's comeback period in the 1950s, after the reputed scandal of her wartime love affair with a Nazi and her temporary eclipse by Christian Dior.

For all the canny marketing that lay behind it, the 2.55 was a deeply personal creation, its every detail seemingly swathed in the not-so-private mythology of Gabriele 'Coco' Chanel (1883–1971). The diamond quilting is said to have been variously inspired by the jackets of stable lads and stained-glass windows of the abbey near her convent school, the burgundy lining by the colour of her school uniform, and the hand-braided chain strap by the key chains that dangled from the waists of the nuns… The Catholic-tinged aura of sinful luxury is compounded when one discovers that the zippered compartment in the front flap is said to be a reference to a secret place in her own handbag where she kept her billets-doux.

And the code-like name? Well, it comes as something of a relief to learn that this merely records the date of its creation: February 1955.

The 2.55 was nonetheless revolutionary in its practicality, enabling women to carry a handbag with their hands free. Here the actress Mia Farrow sports a 2.55 on the set of *Rosemary's Baby* (1968).

KELLY BAG

Hermès

The Kelly bag is perhaps *the* iconic bag of the twentieth century – its combination of demure simplicity and unabashed luxury makes it the epitome of classic style. With its clean trapezoid body, graceful arced handle, shallow flap and signature locking belt, the Kelly bag has endured for more than half a century.

Despite its celebrity status through the years, the birth of the bag was muted. Originally designed in the 1930s by Robert Dumas-Hermès (1898–1978), the bag was, for all its exquisite craftsmanship, eminently practical – a refined kind of travel accessory for the automobile age. It took the glamour of a Hollywood movie star to transform it into an international trendsetting must-have. In 1956 the supremely elegant Grace Kelly, recently married to the Prince of Monaco, was scarcely out of the media, and in almost every photograph she appeared with one or another of her beloved Hermès bags. Here was a golden marketing opportunity, so Hermès negotiated with the Monaco royal family to rename the bag in the princess's honour.

In subsequent decades the Kelly spawned a whole family of variants – in some eight sizes, 20 different materials and a rainbow of colours and patterns. The Birkin bag (see page 62) is in reality little more than an upscale Kelly. Craftsmanship has remained key, however, to the Kelly's cachet – lavished on every detail, from the double saddle-stitching and goatskin interior to the four little square feet at its base. With a price tag running well into the thousands and a waiting list to match, the Kelly bag remains resolutely an object of desire.

Modesty or savvy product placement? Newlyweds Grace Kelly and Prince Rainier III of Monaco arrive in New York. Princess Grace carries her Hermès bag in front of her, seemingly to disguise her pregnancy.

PLASTIC SHOPPING BAG

1960
Sten Gustaf Thulin
for Celloplast

The 27th of March 1962 saw a baleful moment in the history of the environment. On that day the US Patent Office granted the Swedish plastics company Celloplast a patent for 'a continuous tube-like packaging material which is constructed and adapted to be divided into individual bags at the point of packaging'. The jargon obscures its momentousness, for the subject of the patent was nothing less than the first one-piece lightweight plastic grocery bag, the invention of Swedish engineer Sten Gustaf Thulin.

Armed with worldwide patents, Celloplast quickly established manufacturing plants across Europe and the United States. The company did not enjoy its monopoly for long. In 1977 the US petrochemical giant Mobil overturned the 1962 patent, and various home-grown companies were able to exploit the bag's potential instead. In the early 1980s two US supermarket chains, Safeway and Kroger, finally abandoned the traditional paper grocery bag (see page 12) and enthusiastically embraced its futuristic alternative.

In its heyday the polyethylene bag seemed just like any other phenomenon of the plastics age. In its country of origin, for example, consumers were filling their households with cheap, durable plastic goods – cheering, optimistic symbols of Sweden's rapid transition from rural to industrial state. A post-plastics hangover was inevitable. By the late 1990s the environmental damage caused by the quietly indestructible plastic shopping bag had made it public enemy number one, and new, greener alternatives were being sought.

In 1960 the plastic bag was an ingenious innovation. Who, back then, could have guessed that it would become one of the banes of today's environment?

46

NUCLEAR FOOTBALL

Could this be the most dangerous handbag in the world? Nothing sums up the terror and paranoia of the Cold War better than the Nuclear Football, the black leather case containing the nuclear codes that, even today, is (nearly) always just a few feet away from the President of the United States. Instituted by John F. Kennedy in the wake of the 1962 Cuban Missile Crisis, the case contains not only the 'go codes', but also the ominously named Black Book, which lists the retaliatory options open to the US President (summed up by one commentator, with gruesome humour, as 'rare, medium or well done').

The Football is, in fact, not one case but two, for inside the black leather 'jacket' is a specially adapted Zero Halliburton (see page 28), the iconic, near-indestructible aluminium attaché case. There are, moreover, three Footballs, not one. The first is kept in the White House, the second with the vice president and the third, the most famous, discreetly carted around by a military aide, the 'carrier', who more often than not is chained to the case like a prisoner to his ball and chain.

The elaborate security that surrounds the Football is meant to be failsafe, although once or twice things have not gone quite to plan. President Clinton, for instance, once managed to leave a 'carrier' behind at a meeting and the officer had to walk the half-mile back to the White House. It must have been a heavy burden indeed.

The 'Doomsday bag'. The black attaché known as the Nuclear Football is a sober reminder of the power and responsibility held by the President of the United States.

SHOPPER

Bonnie Cashin

'Make things as lightweight as possible – as simple as possible – as punchy as possible – as inexpensive as possible.' This was the manifesto of the American designer Bonnie Cashin (1907–2000), a key figure in the development of forward-thinking fashion in the mid-twentieth century and a pioneer of designer ready-to-wear.

During the 1960s Cashin began to work for the New York leather goods company Coach, producing a series of hardwearing, understated bags that went out of their way to meet the needs of busy working women. Teaming bold, simple shapes and gorgeous ice-cream colours (mustard, pistachio green, candy pink), these were bags that were meant to be used, not shown – carried on crowded commuter trains and teeming city streets, flung into supermarket baskets or tossed onto the back seats of cars. In short, they were the perfect bags for the liberated women of the Betty Friedan generation.

The leather shopper was the undoubted star of the Coach range. Available in three sizes and in a range of vivid colours, these bags shouted practicality and style. They were perfect, too, for 'layering' – Cashin believed that carrying one bag was never enough, as a woman had so many different lives to lead, so many different roles to perform.

A small closed shopper by Bonnie Cashin. Cashin's candy-coloured shoppers for Coach were revolutionary because of their lack of a frame, unusual at this time.

COCKTAIL BAG

late 1960s
Emilio Pucci

By the late 1950s the Italian take on modernity – in the form of cappuccino bars and Vespas, Fellini films and full-lipped, voluptuous actresses – was being exported worldwide. Italian fashion, too, was at the global cutting edge, uniting slick, urbane styling, beautiful materials and superlative craftsmanship to create crisp, eye-catching clothes and accessories.

The aristocratic Florentine designer Emilio Pucci (1914–92) perhaps best caught the Italianate spirit of the 1960s. His instantly recognizable clothes and handbags combined sharp silhouettes with brilliant psychedelic patterning that echoed the Pop Art and Op Art movements of the decade. It was only fitting, too, that Pucci should add his own vivid note to some of the iconic moments of the time – in 1962 Marilyn Monroe was buried in a chartreuse Pucci dress, while almost ten years later the designer's striking three-bird motif was used for the patch of the Apollo 15 moon mission.

This cocktail bag from the late 1960s is gorgeous, classic Pucci. The bold colours, ostentatious gold fittings and slick form may take the design to the edge of (expensive) kitsch. But add a splash of Mediterranean sunshine and Sophia Loren's supple, bronzed arm, and the picture is complete.

Dazzling colours, lustrous hardware and bold shapes are some of the hallmarks of the classic, groovy Pucci bag.

METAL SHOULDER BAG

Fashion, like any art, has its *enfants terribles*, and in the 1960s the role undoubtedly belonged to the Spanish-born but French-raised designer Paco Rabanne (1934–). Rabanne was both an innovator and an iconoclast, whose first haute couture collection famously featured 'Twelve Unwearable Dresses'. Rabanne engineered, rather than designed, his clothes, using unconventional, recalcitrant materials such as plastic and metal to create simple shift dresses that were uncomfortable to wear, but made a high-concept splash on the runway. Space-age aesthetics and fetishistic sexuality were Rabanne's *raisons d'être*.

Rabanne applied the same engineering skills to accessories, and this aluminium shoulder bag became highly sought after. The bag was intended as an irreverent riposte to Chanel's classic padded 2.55 shoulder bag (see page 42), the quasi-mythical status of which Rabanne debunked by replacing Coco's gold chain with a toilet pull-chain. The result was remote indeed from the shimmering, silken metal mesh bags of the 1920s (see page 22). But, even as it celebrated the industrial, the brutalist, the unconventional and the extreme, the bag achieved a kind of high-modern glamour against the odds. With sure-fire inevitability the anti-icon became an icon.

Paco Rabanne's metal shoulder bag was an ironic and iconoclastic take on a classic – Chanel's 2.55 (see page 42) – and in turn itself became a classic.

55

SPORTS BAG

c.1970
Adidas

During the 1970s sportsmen and women became celebrities – tennis players such as Ilie Nastase and footballers like Pelé were not just international icons, but also role models for the young. Sport was hip and even the least fit wanted a bit of the glamour and lifestyle. Sports style became street style as sporting staples from athletic shoes and baseball caps to the humble sweatband began to seep down into everyday dress and fashions – whether in the form of hip-hop cool or discotheque chic.

In Britain the Adidas sports bag was a must-have youth accessory of the 1970s, beloved by comprehensive (state) schoolboys ... and girls.

Until then not usually seen outside a gym or a football changing room, the sports bag, too, became a ubiquitous street item, a pop culture statement of urban savvy. The bags vaunted their utilitarianism – the durable synthetic rubber, unfussy shape, bold colours, contrasting trims and strong logos all helped to turn these unassuming bags into a youth-driven 'mod revival' cult. These were fashion items that even the most blustering of schoolboys could admit to coveting.

JANE BIRKIN'S BASKET c.1970

In the early 1970s the British actress and singer Jane Birkin was rarely photographed without a wicker basket swinging from one arm and a baby – the infant Charlotte Gainsbourg – clasped in the crook of the other. Flower Power was at its zenith and Birkin, star of the film *Blow-Up* (1966) and sultry singer of 'Je t'aime… moi non plus' (1969), straddled the two key feminine stereotypes of the time: wide-eyed child of nature and space age femme fatale. Her dress sense was notorious – she wore the shortest of minis, the most diaphanous of dresses and hardly ever a bra. The wicker basket brought a surprising touch of bucolic charm to such ensembles, even when teamed with gorgeous, decadent fur.

Birkin's playful adoption of the basket was not without precedent. The basket, of course, is a kind of handbag – thousands of year old – but it did not become a fashion item until the late eighteenth century, as an accessory for sophisticated *Parisiennes* playing at being simple shepherdesses. The basket's clear architectural shapes, down-to-earth functionality and truth to materials made it a mark of natural simplicity for the spoiled and pampered ladies who had read too much Rousseau.

By the 1980s Birkin had adopted a different style, the unashamed luxury and ostentation of the massive Hermès bag named after her (see page 62).

Back to nature: actress and chanteuse Jane Birkin with one of her hallmark wicker baskets in 1972.

BLACK NYLON BAG

1978
Prada

Leather is the quintessential material of the luxury handbag – the more rare and supple the leather, the more desirable the bag and the higher the accompanying price tag. However, in the late 1970s, shortly after she had taken over the running of the family firm, Miuccia Prada (1949–) threw this vulgarly sybaritic equation out of the window. She introduced a range of totes and backpacks made of that most unglamorous of materials, nylon – a synthetic 'silk replacement' whose highest claim to fashion fame had hitherto been the nylon stocking first created in 1940. The hefty price tag, of course, remained.

A former Communist, feminist and student of mime with a PhD in political science, Miuccia Prada was initially an unwilling apprentice to the fashion industry and was determined to go her own way. For her, luxury was to be found not in ostentation – anyone could do that – but in an almost monastic simplicity and utilitarian rigour. The black nylon bag was the ultimate statement of the new Prada aesthetic, an object of absolute discretion whose cool modernity was nonetheless rooted in the time-honoured craft traditions of northern Italy. This was luxury in the abstract – fashion as *arte povera*.

The black nylon Prada bag soon gathered its own particular lustre, of course. By the mid-1980s, it would become, in its various incarnations – handbags, totes and rucksacks – a fashionista must-have.

Luxury in the abstract – the original black nylon Prada bag. The silver trimming and handles are its sole concession to worldliness.

BIRKIN BAG

1984
Hermès

'It's not a bag, it's a Birkin,' purrs the supercilious salesman when *Sex and the City*'s Samantha exclaims at the five-year waiting list for the world's most coveted handbag. Five years is a fanciful exaggeration, but it suggests something of the Birkin's potency as a status symbol. Named after the actress and singer Jane Birkin, it is the Shangri-La of the bag world – always just out of reach, glimpsed on the arms of the world's wealthiest, most fashionable women.

Is it possible to have too much luxury? Neither the exclusive French fashion label nor its well-heeled clientele seems to think so. Like its ancestor, the almost as illustrious but smaller Kelly (see page 44), the Birkin is created by a dedicated craftsman, who will lavish no less than 48 hours on its making. Prices run from just over £4,000 to £80,000, depending on the rarity of the leather and the custom additions. Saltwater crocodile, diamonds or silvery-white palladium hardware are currently among the more recherché options.

And Samantha? She got her handbag, of course, but only by lying through her teeth. She would be horrified by the nonchalance of Lady Gaga, who, on a visit to Tokyo in 2010, was photographed with a snowy-white Birkin that had been graffitied with Japanese characters. Luxury, in the end, must subvert itself.

Hermès' oversized Birkin bag is said to have been designed after the company chairman met the actress Jane Birkin on a plane. Accidentally scattering the contents of her crammed Hermès datebook across the floor, Birkin complained bitterly about its size. Her wish was his command, and the Birkin was born.

MESSENGER BAG

1989
Timbuk2

San Francisco has a good claim to be the home of the bicycle messenger – the first modern courier company, Sparkie's, was founded there in 1945, several decades before the global explosion of the messenger business during the 1980s. The City by the Bay can also lay claim to being the host for one of the first, and undoubtedly one of the most iconic, companies to make the messenger (or courier) bag – Timbuk2, founded in 1989.

A version of the waterproof single-strapped backpack can be traced back to 1950s New York, where it was used by the city's linesmen to carry their tools while scrambling up telegraph poles. New York bicycle messengers seem to have adopted the bags at the beginning of the 1980s. Over on the West Coast, Timbuk2 – or Scumbags, as it was originally named – was born out of the messenger subculture itself, as it was the brainchild of the seasoned courier Rob Honeycutt. The bags' distinctive three-panel design, eye-catching 'swirl' logo and reputation for durability quickly won them a fanatical following among San Francisco's vibrant courier community.

During the 1990s the messenger bag quickly migrated into wider society as a youthful urban fashion accessory. Couriers were fit and cool, and the bags' practical design, slick looks and tough fabrics made them just as appropriate for the sidewalk as for the street.

Right and below: The tricoloured Timbuk2 was one of the first messenger bags, arising out of the bicycle courier culture of the late 1970s. By the 1990s the messenger bag had been adopted as trendy streetwear across the globe.

MARGARET THATCHER'S BAG

1980s
Ferragamo

Winston Churchill had his cigar, Margaret Thatcher her handbag… During the 1980s the Conservative British prime minister rarely appeared without a glossy handbag gracefully hung over one arm. It became so synonymous with her charismatic, not to say browbeating, presence that one Cabinet member is said to have quipped while waiting for Thatcher's arrival at a meeting, 'Why don't we start? The handbag is here.'

A verb, 'to handbag' – meaning to treat ruthlessly or insensitively – was even coined in the Iron Lady's 'honour'. The handbag, that most feminine and placid of accessories, had graduated to full-blown superpower. It was an apt-enough attribute for the UK's first female prime minister and a woman able to wield both 'masculine' strength and 'feminine' sex appeal.

Thatcher's favourite handbags were by Ferragamo. Classic in design, beautifully crafted and with a restraint suggestive of the PM's pent-up energy and resolve, each was a bag like an unlit bomb. The enduring fascination with both Thatcher and her handbag was in evidence in 2000 when one of her Ferragamo bags sold at a charity auction for more than £100,000 ($150,000). Now *that* is soft power.

Right: Margaret Thatcher sits for her sculpted portrait (2002) by Neil Simmons. On the floor beside her is one of the 'Iron Lady's' many Ferragamo bags.

Below: A crocodile-skin Ferragamo bag with a gilt metal *gancino* logo fastening.

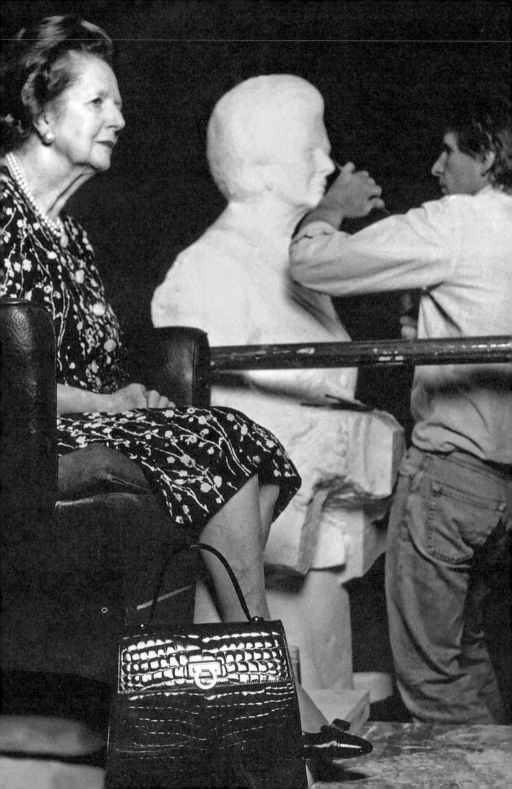

SATCHEL

1992
Bill Amberg

What kind of bag should a woman carry to work? Something stylish and graceful? The danger there is that it may send out the wrong kind of signal – too frivolous, too unprofessional. Something huge and practical, then? Practical is good, but no one wants to be seen lugging about some bulging monstrosity. Back in the 1980s the American designer Donna Karan came up with one influential solution – the satellite bag tucked away inside a briefcase – but that, in reality, is no solution at all. Why, after all, make life so complicated? And in any case, surely a work bag *can* be both stylish and practical?

One of the UK's foremost leather designers, Bill Amberg (1961–) always aims straight down the middle, seeking out the common ground between function and fashion. Indeed, for him there is no real contradiction between these two aspects. 'My personal preference has always been for the function-meets-beauty side of things,' he states. This beautiful red satchel nicely illustrates his point. Nothing could be more practical or simple than the traditional school satchel (see page 36). But what transforms this bag from dull everyday staple to luxurious necessity is the creamy softness of the leather, the refinement in the detail and the gorgeous (but not *too* gorgeous) colour.

Amberg's mantra, 'Bags that you can wear – not a bag that wears you', is not just sound advice when choosing a work bag; it is sound advice for any bag.

Sometimes it is the quality of the craftsmanship, rather than any especial innovation in design, that marks out a 'classic' bag, as in this satchel by the British designer Bill Amberg.

INRO BAG

1993
Nathalie Hambro

The handbag is not just about practicality, or even luxury; it is about pleasure – the aesthetic, spiritual and, indeed, fetishistic pleasure that can be had from a beautiful object, especially one that is held in such intimate relation to the body. The handbag is also about wonder. A woman's handbag is a receptacle of mysteries, a Pandora's box of all things feminine, an intoxicating place of secrets and desires.

The handbag as art. Nathalie Hambro's intricate handcrafted bag turns an everyday object into something precious and wonderful.

Pleasure and wonder are certainly the hallmarks of the exquisite limited-edition bags made by the London-based designer and writer Nathalie Hambro, part of a generation of British artist-makers who sought to regenerate the craft tradition in the early 1990s. Hambro deals in the elaborate, the recherché and the strange, constructing works that blend art and design, modern materials and painstaking technique and research. The Inro bag is just such an *objet d'art*.

It derives in form and name from the tiny cylindrical Japanese nested caskets that were traditionally worn suspended from a sash and were used to carry personal belongings such as medicines. With its body of stainless-steel gauze, decoration of embossed metal sheeting, and cord of dulled silver, the Inro may at first sight seem a somewhat fastidious and puzzling work. But that is just the point. In an age of ostentatious display and mass-market design, the Inro restores intimacy and idiosyncrasy to the bag.

BUM BAG

1996
Vivienne Westwood
for Louis Vuitton

The bum bag, or fanny pack, is perhaps the least glamorous and most nerdy of all bag genres, for ever doomed to be associated with bewildered-looking tourists or nylon-clad map-reading hikers – or so you might have thought. It is a credit to the genius of British fashion's *grande dame*, Vivienne Westwood (1941–), that, even at the height of the bum bag's popularity in the mid-1990s, she was able at a stroke to sweep away all such connotations with her limited-edition creation for Louis Vuitton.

It is something of a Westwoodian trademark that she can simultaneously cite, celebrate and subvert sartorial tradition in her work. With her Louis Vuitton bum bag – here worn 'correctly' at the rear – she alludes to the Victorian bustle (an enduring obsession in Westwood's work), while also paying homage to the curves of the female body. The *pièce de résistance*, of course, was Westwood's appropriation of Vuitton's signature Monogram canvas, with its discreet *melange* of quatrefoils, flowers and 'LV' monograms – textile shorthand for bourgeois cosmopolitan refinement since the beginning of the century. The design was exactly a hundred years old, and Westwood blew it sky-high.

Vivienne Westwood puts the 'bum' back into the bum bag in this uproarious, clever design from 1996.

FUDGE THE FASHIONISTAS
LET THEM EAT CAKE

1996
Moschino

The Italian label Moschino has continued to deal in the wit and irreverence – as well as the heartfelt anti-establishment fervour – that was the trademark of the company's founder, Franco Moschino (1950–94). And his spirit certainly lives on in this lusciously crafted bag issued two years after his premature death.

During the 1980s Moschino's designs were a breath of fresh air in the stiflingly solipsistic atmosphere of the newly globalized fashion industry. His innovations lay, however, not so much in design – in the creation of new shapes or technologies – but in his uncanny ability simultaneously to create luxury and to send it up. Every fashionista worth their salt would have killed to get hold of a shirt emblazoned with the words: 'A shirt only for fashion victims.' But there was more to all this than mere ironic whimsy – there was genuine passion in the famous 1980s magazine advertisement that harangued readers to 'Stop the Fashion System'.

The Fudge the Fashionistas handbag continues the tricky tightrope walk between the subversion and the perpetuation of consumerism. The imagery of the bag is an allusion to the base gluttony of the 'fashionistas', of course, but the sheer yumminess of the polished calfskin – representing the glossy darkness of the fudge sauce as it oozes down the vanilla cake crumb – threatens to open up an unnerving split in the modern psyche, torn between our idealist and consumerist selves. But that, Franco Moschino would have said, is the point.

Conspicuous consumption. This luscious take on the luxury handbag by Moschino both flaunts and critiques our love affair with high-end consumerism.

BAGUETTE

Contemporary television, like cinema before it, routinely collaborates with the fashion industry to generate glamour and consumerist desire. Nowhere is this more evident, of course, than in the HBO series *Sex and the City* (1998–2004), whose thirty-something heroines endlessly hankered after fashion labels and in so doing propelled them deep into the public consciousness. Jimmy Choo, Manolo Blahnik and the Hermès Birkin (see page 62) all benefited from their promotion in this way.

The Fendi baguette was yet another. All it took was Carrie Bradshaw to exclaim, 'I'm homeless! I'll be a bag lady. A Fendi bag lady, but a bag lady!' and the exquisite Italian clutch bag became an icon overnight – the first global 'It bag', no less.

As a design statement, the baguette scarcely needed such crude (but outrageously effective) product placement. Its discreet narrow shape and gorgeous array of colours and materials, all set off by the distinctive double-'F' buckle (designed by Fendi's creative director, Karl Lagerfeld), immediately set it apart from the dismal, minimalist fare then on offer. For all its 00 sizing, the baguette exuded a baroque splendour that recalled the Roman *palazzi* in which its designer, Silvia Fendi (1961–), spent her youth.

Even sans *Sex and the City*, each version of the baguette – and there have been many – remains as fresh-baked and toothsome as ever. Good things do come in small packages.

Two of the many avatars of the Fendi baguette: Zephyr's Whisper (above) and Jungle Fever (below). The richness of patterning and colour is more than a match for the grandiose names.

76

US ARMY MOLLE PACK

1997

Modern soldiers and marines are infinitely more sophisticated fighting machines than their predecessors, requiring 'load-carrying equipment' (LCE) that is fluid, adaptable and comfortable enough to be used in the complex, challenging environments of modern warfare. The current state-of-the-art LCE is the MOLLE system: Modular Lightweight Load-carrying Equipment. First introduced in 1997, it is widely deployed today in conflicts such as those in Iraq and Afghanistan.

Like most other modern products, MOLLE is the result of a long process of market research, technical development, prototyping and testing. Surprisingly, however, much of the initial inspiration for MOLLE came from the commercial off-the-shelf backpack, whose higher, narrower volume provided a better load centre than MOLLE's predecessor, ALICE (All-Purpose Lightweight Individual Carrying Equipment) – crucial when you remember that a modern soldier's load can be as much as 120lb (54kg). Among the innovations of the MOLLE pack are an anatomically shaped plastic internal frame and an improved suspension system with heavily padded shoulder straps.

The pack, or 'ruck', itself is only the main part of a complex modular system that includes what is for the civilian a bewildering array of pouches and fittings. These are attached to a core load-bearing nylon-mesh vest using an innovative webbing system knows as PALS – the Pouch Attachment Ladder System. Acronyms and all, the soldiers' 'bag' has come a long way since the canvas haversack of World War I (see page 20).

Returning US Marines from the 26th Marine Expeditionary Unit unload their MOLLE packs from the USS Shreveport, after arriving at Morehead City, North Carolina, in 2002.

MANBAG/MURSE

late 1990s

Since time immemorial men have carried bags, but conventionally they have always been unshowy and practical. The businessman had his briefcase, the workman his toolbox, the bicycle courier his messenger bag, and so on. A man who carried a bag because it was, God forbid, to some degree decorative ran the terrifying risk of 'compromising' his masculinity.

The tide began to turn in the late 1990s when the fashion industry spotted the potential for a new market, and the terms 'manbag' and 'murse' began to do the rounds. Non-coincidentally, no doubt, this period also saw the birth pangs of the 'metrosexual' male, for whom well-chosen accessories were a high priority. There were jitters, however. In 1999 the US sitcom *Friends* put out an episode in which aspiring actor Joey becomes unhealthily attached to his 'murse' and fails an audition because of it. Even in Manhattan, it seemed, the world was not quite ready for the glamorous peacock male.

Today the manbag is ubiquitous, at least in major cities. While it usually takes the form of a soft leather satchel or an upscale messenger bag, there are the occasional surprises, such as the brown and gold Louis Vuitton clutch once sported by David Beckham. How long will it be, one wonders, before we have the male evening bag?

The manbag is now truly here to stay, as shown in this example from British high-street retailer Topman.

KNIERTJE

1999
Susan Boer

Of all main bag genres, the rucksack is perhaps the most ungainly and the most unfeminine; it is also, however, one of the most practical and comfortable. One design solution to this dilemma is to soften or deconstruct the rucksack (see page 104). Another – the route taken by the Utrecht-based Dutch designer Susan Boer (1959–) – is to pare it back to its essential form.

Rigorous design and superlative craftsmanship enable Dutch designer Susan Boer to pare back the rucksack to its purest form.

The main body of Boer's Kniertje is simple. Made from three pieces of leather saddle-stitched together, the bag creates an elegant 'apostrophe' shape that fits snugly into the back of the wearer. A long, tongue-like flap and a pocket like an upturned pouch are otherwise the only embellishments in a piece that, in the purity of its colour and shape, borders on abstraction – which is only fitting for a bag crafted in a city famous for its associations with the Dutch design movement de Stijl.

Bags, unlike other accessories such as hats and shoes, very often have a 'semi-detached' relationship with their wearer, dangling freely from an arm, wrist or shoulder. The Kniertje, however, melds ergonomically with the body, to create a single harmonious form.

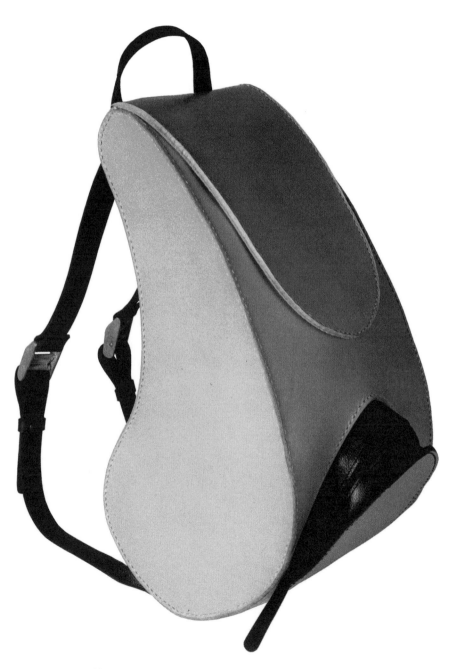

QUEEN'S HANDBAG

Launer

During the British Queen's state visit to Italy in 2000, Her Majesty's fashion sense came under close scrutiny from the Italian press. Usually much derided for what is considered to be her staid and rather pompous style, the Queen suddenly became the best-dressed woman in Milan. It was, however, her discreet, well-mannered handbag that drew the most attention.

One of Italy's leading newspapers, *La Repubblica*, even carried a front-page story entitled 'Ode to the Queen's handbag': 'There it is,' the article raved. 'That disturbing object, firmly attached to her left forearm. The secret of her regality is in that little royal but so ordinary accessory.'

That 'royal but so ordinary' accessory was in fact made by Launer, a well-established maker of leather goods based in Britain's industrial heartland, the Midlands, and, off and on, a holder of a royal warrant since the 1960s. The Launer 'brand' – it scarcely merits the term – is as quiet and as reserved as its beautifully crafted bags. Luxury here is the polar opposite of bling. The calf, lizard and ostrich leathers are all turned and hand-machined with the maximum of attention to detail, but with the minimum of 'designer' fuss. The gold-plated fittings – including the company's crossed-rope emblem – are the closest concessions to ostentation.

The other great obsession of the Italian press was what the Queen actually carried in that handbag. What on earth, they wondered, could this woman, who has everything, possibly *need* to carry around with her? Her lipstick, of course, Buckingham Palace laconically revealed.

The Queen's carries a patent-leather Launer handbag during her state visit to Italy in 2000. For all its quiet modesty, the handbag caused a storm.

MULTI STEM CLASSIC SHOULDER BAG

2001
Orla Kiely

Orla Kiely, the London-based design firm headed by the Irish-born designer Orla Kiely and her husband, Dermott Rowan, is one of the great success stories of the 2000s. The cleanly designed clothes, accessories and household furnishings, featuring fresh 1950s-, 1960s- and 1970s-inspired prints, are sold across the globe, their cheerful colours and playful optimism flying in the face of economic gloom.

Multi Stem, one of the most popular variations of the Stem motif, which sums up the breezy, happy-go-lucky styling of Kiely's handbag designs.

In 1997 Kiely, who had initially trained in knitwear, set up a design studio in south London. The breakthrough came in 2001, with the production of a series of soft fabric bags that featured her now-famous Stem pattern. Against the backdrop of the sullen raincloud-black handbags then usually on offer, the Stem design – with its nod towards the abstract mid-century modern textiles of designers such as Lucienne Day – was like a cool summer breeze. To Kiely's surprise, the style even translated well into her winter range, with the use of darker tones – brown and cream, dark khaki and olive, Bordeaux and pink – and, daringly, laminated cotton, hitherto associated with wipe-clean tablecloths.

The Stem design has since become the signature pattern of the Orla Kiely brand and has developed unlimited variations in a range of scales and multiple colours. In 2009 Kiely created a special edition, Butterfly Stem, for the British cancer charity Maggie's.

LIPS CLUTCH

2004
Lulu Guinness

If you could use just one word to describe the handbags of the British designer Lulu Guinness (1960–) it would have to be 'feminine'. Whether in the form of flower buckets, birdcages or quaint English cottages, or in more conventional or conservative shapes and styles, these are purses that revel in prettiness and charm – miles away, indeed, from the brassy ostentation of many of Guinness's contemporaries. One of her inspirations was her mother, whose own handbag rituals involved 'gloves, the smell of powder, [and] putting on lipstick 15 times a day'. In a Lulu Guinness bag the clipped, meticulous glamour of the 1950s is reborn.

The Lips clutch is an apt leitmotif for the Lulu Guinness brand, evoking as it does the bee-stung mouths and *über*-femininity of 1950s stars such as Marilyn Monroe. Feminine glamour is not the whole story here, however. As in much of Guinness's work, the Lips clutch also shows the designer's love of surrealism, of the most playful and light-hearted kind. It is not too much to see in this glossy, dainty evening bag a tribute in microcosm to Salvador Dalí's infamous, outrageous Mae West Lips sofa, a creation of the late 1930s.

Right: Lulu Guinness is one of the darlings of handbag aficionados. Her quirky, playful designs, such as the iconic Lips clutch, have made them a contemporary collectable. Below: The Lips clutch gets the celebrity treatment from English supermodel and actress Agyness Deyn.

BOOTBAG

2004
Saskia Marcotti

The contemporary obsession with the handbag as the ultimate fashion and consumer statement reached its apogee – some might say nadir – when, for Christmas 2008, footballer-cum-celebrity David Beckham gave his wife, Victoria, a diamond-encrusted 'Himalayan' version of the famous Birkin bag (see page 62). It cost him £80,000 ($116,000). The handbag undoubtedly looked gorgeous, but for some the inflated price tag and the associated inflated egos took away much of its silvery sheen.

The Bootbag is the perfect antidote to such vainglory. A paintbox-coloured children's rubber Wellington boot is transformed through the simple device of piercing two horizontal handles into either side of its shaft. The Bootbag was designed by the young Belgian-Italian Saskia Marcotti (1986–) – who was just 18 at the time – as one of the launch products of the witty Belgian design label Vlaemsch. Mass-produced and marketed at just €35 (£30, or $44), it combines chunky looks and topsy-turvy charm, making it an instant street classic.

From time to time contemporary design, with its ever-present tendency towards pomposity and hyperbole, needs such playful irreverence to keep its feet firmly on the ground.

Belgian designer Saskia Marcotti undercuts all the self-importance of contemporary handbag design with her witty, smile-inducing Bootbag.

I'M NOT A PLASTIC BAG

2007
Anya Hindmarch

Can a bag *really* change the world? What can possibly be so meaningful about a bag that its very existence can improve the quality of our daily lives, let alone alter the destiny of our planet? Of all the bags in this book – beautiful, iconic and downright desirable as they are – it is perhaps the simple canvas tote by Anya Hindmarch (1968–) that has the best claim to the title 'Most World-changing Bag'. Yet it is also one of the cheapest: 'A £5 It Bag!', as a celebrity magazine screamed.

Created in collaboration with the British environmental charity We Are What We Do, the Hindmarch bag set out to wean us off our addiction to the plastic bag by making the homey canvas shopper seem so much more chic. Nicely designed though it was, the bag in itself was hardly ground-breaking; its marketing, by contrast, was inspired. Even before its launch, photographs of celebrities such as Keira Knightley sporting the bag had seeped into the media, and such was the hype that in Britain thousands queued outside supermarkets in the desperate hope of buying one.

A backlash was inevitable. Its detractors questioned whether the bag was really so green. Why was it made in China and why was it not made from organic cotton? Yes, it had its faults, but then no bag is perfect (except perhaps an Hermès), and in its own small and lovable way the Hindmarch bag really did change the world.

Anya Hindmarch's I'm Not a Plastic Bag attracted both admirers and detractors as it set out to end our ingrained addiction to the plastic shopping bag.

THE UNIQUE BAG PROJECT

2008
Hikaru Matsumura
for Issey Miyake

In today's supersaturated marketplace, the quest for originality can sometimes seem futile. This season's must-have glossy black bag may not look so different from last season's, and the cross-pollination, not to say plagiarism, between even the most exalted brands can mean that it ends up being hard to tell even a Gucci and a Pucci apart. There is very little new under the sun. The true test of a good (or bad) handbag lies in the quality of the craftsmanship, the obsessiveness of the detailing and the fundamental passion that underpins the design.

In the Unique Bag Project, first launched as a brand in 2007, the Japanese designer Hikaru Matsumura (1964–) has striven to create a series of bags whose uniqueness lies in the sheer depth of the craftsmanship. Gloves have previously provided inspiration for bags: Moschino, for example, created a tongue-in-cheek bag in the form of a cherry-red boxing glove back in 2001. Matsumura, however, has taken an altogether more authentic approach, marrying his precise creative vision with the craft skills of a baseball glove manufacturer in Osaka, Japan.

The result is a curiously anthropomorphic and even fetishistic form – the intricate stitching is vaguely suggestive of a laced-up bodice. The passion here, though, is in the detail, from the elaborately pierced and stitched central panel to the laced, nipped-in sides. Who needs originality when you can have uniqueness?

The baseball glove provides the inspiration for Hikaru Matsumura's Unique Bag Project.

HOME TOTE

2009
Hussein Chalayan

Since the 1990s the plastic shopping bag (see page 46) has become the *bête noire* of the environmental movement. Handed out willy-nilly in supermarkets across the globe, the seemingly indestructible plastic bag consumes vast quantities of petrochemicals, is responsible for the death of millions of animals and, on land and sea, is the unsightly, toxic symbol of our throw-away culture. Despite international moves to inhibit or even ban its use, tens of billions of plastic shopping bags are still being produced every year – although estimates vary, in many countries it amounts to some 300 bags per year per person.

There are encouraging signs of change. The plastic bag is fast becoming anathema, and the canvas shopper – once the mainstay of the market-going housewife – has made a comeback. British/Turkish Cypriot Hussein Chalayan (1970–) produced this handsome printed cotton canvas tote in aid of the environmental initiative HOME. Throwing off the somewhat fusty image of the shopper, it shows us that it can be chic to be green. Chalayan, whose career has always combined avant-garde design with support for progressive causes, uses the bag to promote another issue, too – the accelerating extinction rate threatening some 40 per cent of the planet's known animal species.

Chic to be green. Hussein Chalayan's HOME tote depicts some of the world's endangered species; the blanked-out spaces represent the thousands of species already lost.

ALEXA BAG

Mulberry

Since the early 1970s the Mulberry brand has been the purveyor of a certain kind of nostalgic English style – the country house world of tweeds, Wellington boots and Labradors, of hunting, shooting and fishing – that was perfectly summed up in the company's discreet mulberry tree logo. Mulberry's founder, Roger Saul, started out by designing leather goods such as belts and chokers for London high-end fashion stores such as Biba, and within a couple of years was meeting orders from the likes of Bloomingdale's in New York. In the 1980s the Mulberry planner, an upmarket version of the Filofax, became a must-have yuppy accessory.

In more recent times Mulberry has begun to throw off what had become a rather stilted and stodgy image, and, like Burberry before it, is now finding favour with a younger, hipper crowd. The Mulberry Alexa bag may hark back to the capacious 'poacher's bags' with which the company originally made its name – its warm oak colour, soft buffalo leather and sturdy, simple shape root the bag firmly in the English saddlery tradition – but this is unquestionably a contemporary urban bag, albeit one with an eye on the past. There is even, for dressy occasions, a fuzzy leopard-print version in pink. Ditch those wellingtons … a new English style has arrived.

A classic in the making: the Alexa bag is inspired by and named after the British model, presenter and 'It girl' Alexa Chung.

'MINI ON LOCATION' HOLDALL

2009
Paul Smith

Two great British icons of the late twentieth century come together in this quirky canvas holdall – the highly respected designer and retailer Paul Smith (1946–) and the small but feisty Mini Cooper car, the epitome of swinging 1960s pizzazz. Smith's association with the Mini dates back to the late 1990s. In 1998 he collaborated with the car's manufacturer, the Rover Group, on a limited-edition version, inspired by a one-off Mini he had designed for the 1997 Tokyo Motor Show, with bodywork featuring the designer's famous signature motif, incorporating stripes in 86 different colours.

In the 2000s the stripy car began to appear in an innovative series of photographic prints – known as 'Mini on Location' – used on a range of classic Paul Smith accessories, from bags to cufflinks. The striking, surrealistic images staged the rainbow Mini in iconic British settings – Portland Bill lighthouse, the roof of Harrods department store, and, here, a wintry Sherwood Forest, the 'shire wood' of Smith's native county of Nottinghamshire and the legendary home of Robin Hood.

As always with Smith's work, it is the combination of classic style with a humorous or characterful twist that lifts the bag out of the run-of-the-mill. Quality craftsmanship, too – evident everywhere here, from the purple inner lining to the brown leather handles and trim – helps to create the perfect holdall for the modern gentleman.

British icons collide in this zany but classic holdall by Paul Smith.

'ACCORDION' HANDBAG

2010
Lie Sang Bong

The handbag is the most sculptural of fashion accessories. Unlike hats (which meld with the face) and shoes (which with any luck stay put on the feet) the handbag can just as often be spotted alone, set down on a table or chair as it can be seen swinging from its owner's arm. Shape, structure and silhouette are thus key qualities of any handbag – from the hard-edged lozenge of a Wilardy Rocket (see page 40) to the more relaxed, 'melting' shape of an Alexa (see page 98).

In terms of shape, handbag design usually conforms to tried-and-tested formulas. The South Korean designer Lie Sang Bong, however, dares to be different.

The shape of a bag can tell us something about the wearer, her personality and mood, and even the age in which she lives. Uptight style queens love hard-edged glamour, while laid-back bohemians prefer the unstructured and casual. Capacious bags are for hard times when we all have too much to do; small ones are for more frivolous, free-spirited times when we are hardly out of our dancing shoes.

What then should we make of the Korean designer Lie Sang Bong's 'Accordion' bag? With its high-concept form and sleek gothic looks, this bag makes a statement that is bold but complex. Dramatic? Erotic? Dystopian, even? You choose. We live, it seems, in a complex, fragmented age.

DAYSACK

The backpack, or rucksack, is one of the most ancient types of bag, used by hunter-gatherers who needed to have their hands free as they wandered through primordial forests in search of prey. In modern times the rucksack has long been staple military issue (see page 20) and it is understandably the bag of choice of both the long-distance hiker and the student backpacker. Unglamorous and downright ugly though such bags may be, they make the rough-and-tumble of such activities possible.

Sportmax's soft, deconstructed rucksack is the perfect bag for a sweltering summer's day about town.

That the backpack could be stylish, even a style icon, was proved back in the 1980s, when in 1985 Prada launched its black nylon backpack to widespread acclaim. For a while it became the 'It bag' of its time, influencing a whole generation of imitations and variations.

The reverberations from this ground-breaking bag are still felt today, as seen in the beautiful summery rucksack issued by the MaxMara label Sportmax in 2010. There is nothing remotely macho here. The creamy colour, the soft pyramidal shape and the plethora of pockets, relieved by rococo curves and brown leather trimming, create a bag that is as light and frothy as a cappuccino.

Sometimes our lives can feel not so different from those of our hunter-gatherer forebears – you really do need your hands free when negotiating the urban jungle. The natural and age-old solution, of course, is the rucksack.

AMAZONLIFE BOWLING BAG

2010
Vivienne Westwood

Tenpin bowling is enjoyed by millions, so it is no surprise that its bold harlequin colours and 1950s retro styling have sometimes slipped out of the bowling alleys and onto the fashion runway. Two-toned suede bowling shoes and bowling shirts have long been preppy staples, while the chunky two-handled bowling bag has given the world of handbags one of its most striking silhouettes.

Vivienne Westwood (1941–) has created a whole rack of bowling bags – including one in rabbit and another, of course, in her signature tartan – but this black-and-white bag from Westwood's Red Label diffusion is her most overt tribute to bowling's 1950s heritage. It also, by the by, gives expression to the designer's much-publicized political activism. Created in collaboration with the environmental campaigning charity AmazonLife, the bag displays a '+5°' logo to push home the message about global warming. The bag's political engagement goes beyond mere sloganeering, however – the canvas is organic and the rubber is of the wild Amazonian variety. And unlike most other bags in this book, this practical, preppy daybag could even double up for a night down at the alleys.

Bag with a message. Vivienne Westwood makes a plea about climate stage with this slick retro-style bowling bag.

INDEX

PICTURE CREDITS

CREDITS

First published in 2011
by Conran Octopus Ltd
in association with
The Design Museum

Conran Octopus Ltd
a part of Octopus Publishing
Group, Endeavour House,
189 Shaftesbury Avenue,
London WC2H 8JY
www.octopusbooks.co.uk

An Hachette UK Company
www.hachette.co.uk

Distributed in the US by
Hachette Book Group USA
237 Park Avenue
New York NY 10017 USA

Distributed in Canada by
Canadian Manda Group
165 Dufferin Street
Toronto, Ontario, Canada
M6K 3H6

Reprinted in 2011 and 2012

Text copyright ©
Conran Octopus Ltd 2011
Design and layout copyright
© Conran Octopus Ltd 2011

British Library Cataloguing-
in-Publication Data.
A catalogue record for
this book is available
from the British Library.

Text written by:
Robert Anderson

Publisher:
Lorraine Dickey
Consultant Editor:
Deyan Sudjic
Managing Editor:
Sybella Marlow
Copy Editor:
Alison Wormleighton
Art Director:
Jonathan Christie
Design:
Untitled
Picture Researcher:
Anne-Marie Hoines
Production:
Caroline Alberti

ISBN: 978 1 84091 570 9
Printed in China